GW01549189

W1

316898

CULTIVATING,

OF A PATH,

AS A LETTING HAPPEN

The Practical Gist of Nagarjuna's Magnum Opus

– 108 Verses to Save the World –

Translated from the Sanskrit by Mike Cross

Cultivating, of a Path, as a Letting Happen
© 2024 by Mike Cross is licensed under
CC BY-NC-ND 4.0.
To view a copy of this license, visit
https://creativecommons.org/licenses/by-nc-nd/4.0/

Prepared and published by Mike Luetchford
Windbell Publications November 2024

Dedicated to the memory of George Grant, 1990 - 2016

Cover: Buddha's Footprints, Brahmavihāra Monastery, Melaka
Photo courtesy of Anandajoti Bikkhu

a-nirodham an-utpādam
an-ucchedam a-śāśvatam |
an-ekārtham a-nānārtham
an-āgamam a-nirgamam ||

yaḥ pratītya-samutpādaṁ
prapañcopaśamaṁ śivam |
deśayām āsa saṁbuddhas
taṁ vande vadatāṁ varam ||

Beyond death and beyond birth
Not nihilist not eternal
Beyond identity beyond difference
Never coming back, or going away

The one who taught the dependently arisen bliss
of the melting away of othering.
The fully awakened one
Among voices, the very choicest –
I cherish him.

āryasatya-parīkṣā

yadi śūnyam idaṁ sarvam
udayo nāsti na vyayaḥ |
caturṇām āryasatyānām
abhāvas te prasajyate |1|

parijñā ca prahāṇaṃ ca
bhāvanā sākṣi-karma ca |
caturṇām āryasatyānām
abhāvān nopapadyate |2|

tad-abhāvān na vidyante
catvāry api phalāni ca |
phalābhāve phala-sthā no
na santi pratipannakāḥ |3|

Exploring The Noble Truths

[Opponent]

If all this is empty,
there is neither arising nor passing.
The nullification follows, for you,
of the four noble truths.

Catching on and dropping off,
cultivating, and seeing for oneself,
following from nullification of the four noble truths,
is impossible.

Following from that nullification,
the four fruits also are not found.
Where the fruits are absent,
neither growers nor garnerers of the fruits exist.

saṃgho nāsti na cet santi
te 'ṣṭau puruṣa-pudgalāḥ |
abhāvāc cāryasatyānāṃ
saddharmo 'pi na vidyate |4|

dharme cāsati saṃghe ca
kathaṃ buddho bhaviṣyati |
evaṃ trīṇy api ratnāni
bruvāṇaḥ pratibādhase |5|

śūnyatāṃ phala-sad-bhāvam
adharmaṃ dharmam eva ca |
sarva-saṃvyavahārāṃś ca
laukikān pratibādhase |6|

When those eight human individuals do not exist,
a sangha does not exist.
From nullification of the noble truths,
again, true dharma also is not realised.

Where dharma and sangha are not existing,
how will there be buddha?

In this way,
you are negating the three treasures themselves
when you speak of...

...emptiness. You are denying:
the reality of the fruits, good and evil,
and all human efforts in the world.

atra brūmaḥ śūnyatāyām
na tvaṃ vetsi prayojanam |
śūnyatāṃ śūnyatārthaṃ ca
tata evaṃ vihanyase |7|

dve satye samupāśritya
buddhānāṃ dharma-deśanā |
loka-saṃvṛti-satyaṃ ca
satyaṃ ca paramārthataḥ |8|

We say on this that you don't know
the purpose in emptiness,
or the nature of emptiness,
or the practical gist of emptiness.
That's why you're striving, like this, in vain.

The dharma-teaching of the buddhas
rests on two truths:
the truth of the convenient fictions of the world,
and ultimate truth.

ye 'nayor na vijānanti
vibhāgaṃ satyayor dvayoḥ |
te tattvaṃ na vijānanti
gambhīre buddha-śāsane |*9*|

vyavahāram anāśritya
paramārtho na deśyate |
paramārtham anāgamya
nirvāṇaṃ nādhigamyate |*10*|

Those who don't know the distinction
between these two truths
do not know how – ineffably – it is,
in the deep teaching of the buddhas.

Without recourse to convention,
the ultimate is not taught.
Without coming to the ultimate,
nirvana is not earned.

vināśayati durdṛṣṭā
śūnyatā manda-medhasam |
sarpo yathā durgṛhīto
vidyā vā duṣprasādhitā |11|

atas ca pratyudāvṛttaṃ
cittaṃ deśayituṃ muneḥ |
dharmaṃ matvāsya dharmasya
mandair duravagāhatām |12|

Emptiness misconstrued
does for the dull-witted,
like a snake badly handled,
or like a spell wickedly cast.

And that's why the Sage's will to teach dharma
was turned back.
He'd seen how hard it would be
for this dharma
to be fathomed by fools.

śūnyatāyām adhilayaṃ
yaṃ punaḥ kurute bhavān |
doṣa-prasaṅgo nāsmākaṃ
sa śūnye nopapadyate |*13*|

sarvaṃ ca yujyate tasya
śūnyatā yasya yujyate |
sarvaṃ na yujyate tasya
śūnyaṃ yasya na yujyate |*14*|

Whatever objection to emptiness
you keep on making,
that blame cannot be attached either to us,
or to what is empty.

For whom emptiness is workable,
everything is workable.
For whom what's empty is not workable,
nothing is workable.

sa tvaṃ doṣān [yad] ātmīyān
asmāsu paripātayan |
aśvam evābhirūḍhaḥ sann
aśvam evāsi vismṛtaḥ |*15*|

svabhāvād yadi bhāvānāṃ
sadbhāvam anupaśyasi |
a-hetu-pratyayān bhāvāṃs
tvam evaṃ sati paśyasi |*16*|

While you're projecting onto us your own faults,
you – mounted high on a horse –
are forgetting that very horse.

If you take the view that the reality of happenings
rests on what exists unto itself,
then you – remaining yourself in such a state –
are seeing happenings bereft of causes or conditions.

kāryaṃ ca kāraṇaṃ caiva
kartāraṃ karaṇaṃ kriyām |
utpādaṃ ca nirodhaṃ ca
phalaṃ ca pratibādhase |*17*|

yaḥ pratītya-samutpādaḥ
śūnyatāṁ tāṁ pracakṣmahe |
sā prajñaptir upādāya
pratipat saiva madhyamā |*18*|

You are denying: practice as end
and practice as means;
the practitioner, the practising, the work of practice;
and arising and cessation; and the fruit.

Whatever dependent arising there is,
we call that emptiness.
This teaching,
when we're making it our own in practice,
is the only way in – the middle one.

apratītya samutpanno

dharmaḥ kaś-cin na vidyate |

yasmāt tasmād aśūnyo' pi

dharmaḥ kaś-cin na vidyate |*19*|

yady aśūnyam idaṃ sarvam

udayo nāsti na vyayaḥ |

caturṇām āryasatyānām

abhāvas te prasajyate |*20*|

No independently arising reality
is realised at all.
On which grounds, therefore,
no non-empty reality, again,
is realised at all.

If all this is not empty,
There is neither arising nor passing.
The nullification follows, for you,
of the four noble truths.

apratītya samutpannaṃ
kuto duḥkhaṃ bhaviṣyati |
anityam uktaṃ duḥkhaṃ hi
tat svābhāvye na vidyate |*21*|

svabhāvato vidyamānaṃ
kiṃ punaḥ samudeṣyate |
tasmāt samudayo nāsti
śūnyatāṃ pratibādhataḥ |*22*|

How will suffering happen
that is arisen independently?
Suffering, after all,
is said to be impermanent.
Where the existent exists unto itself,
that is not experienced.

On the grounds of what exists unto itself,
how will the now being suffered
be caused again to come together?
On those grounds,
for one denying emptiness,
there is no coming together.

na nirodhaḥ svabhāvena
sato duḥkhasya vidyate |
svabhāva-paryavasthānān
nirodhaṃ pratibādhase |*23*|

svābhāvye sati mārgasya
bhāvanā nopapadyate |
athāsau bhāvyate mārgaḥ
svābhāvyaṃ te na vidyate |*24*|

The cessation, of real and present suffering,
isn't witnessed happening by itself.
By holding firm to what sustains itself
you are denying cessation.

Where the self-sustaining is sustaining itself,
cultivating, of a path, doesn't happen.
Or else, where that path is cultivated,
self-sufficiency, as you would have it,
is not found.

yadā duḥkhaṃ samudayo
nirodhaś ca na vidyate |
mārgo duḥkha-nirodham tvām
katamam prāpayiṣyati |*25*|

svabhāvenāparijñānaṃ
yadi tasya punaḥ katham |
parijñānaṃ nanu kila
svabhāvaḥ samavasthitaḥ |*26*|

When suffering, coming together, and cessation
are not witnessed,
what cessation of suffering
will the path lead you to attain?

For one whose lack of understanding is intrinsic,
how is catching on ever possible?
Isn't what exists intrinsically
supposed to be settled?

prahāṇa-sākṣātkaraṇe
bhāvanā caivam eva te |
parijñāvan na yujyante
catvāry api phalāni ca |27|

svabhāvenānadhigataṃ
yat phalaṃ tat punaḥ katham |
śakyaṃ samadhigantuṃ syāt
svabhāvaṃ parigṛhṇataḥ |28|

In exactly the same way,
dropping off, realising in practice, and cultivating
– like catching on –
are unworkable for you.
And so too are the four fruits.

How might it ever be possible,
for one embracing what happens by itself,
to earn that fruit
which the self-sufficient
have never earned?

phalābhāve phala-sthā no
na santi pratipannakāḥ |
saṃgho nāsti na cet santi
te 'ṣṭau puruṣa-pudgalāḥ |*29*|

abhāvāc cāryasatyānāṃ
sad-dharmo 'pi na vidyate |
dharme cāsati saṃghe ca
kathaṃ buddho bhaviṣyati |*30*|

Where the fruits are absent,
neither growers nor garnerers of the fruits exist.
When those eight human individuals do not exist,
a sangha does not exist.

Again, from nullification of the noble truths,
true dharma also is not realised.
Where dharma and sangha are not existing,
how will buddha happen?

apratītyāpi bodhiṃ ca
tava buddhaḥ prasajyate |
apratītyāpi buddhaṃ ca
tava bodhiḥ prasajyate |*31*|

yaś cābuddhaḥ svabhāvena
sa bodhāya ghaṭann api |
na bodhisattva-caryāyāṃ
bodhiṃ te 'dhigamiṣyati |*32*|

And yet for you it follows
that there is a buddha, an awakened one,
independently of awakening.
And for you it follows that there is bodhi,
awakening, independently of an awakened one.

And whoever in your scheme
is intrinsically unawakened,
strive as he might towards awakening
in the conduct of a bodhi-sattva,
will never win awakening.

na ca dharmam adharmaṃ vā
kaś-cij jātu kariṣyati |
kim aśūnyasya kartavyaṃ
svabhāvaḥ kriyate na hi |*33*|

vinā dharmam adharmaṃ ca
phalaṃ hi tava vidyate |
dharmādharma-nimittaṃ ca
phalaṃ tava na vidyate |*34*|

Again, nobody will ever practise good or evil.
What is there about the non-empty to be practised?
What happens by itself, after all,
is not practised.

Without any doing of good, or evil,
for you the fruit is nonetheless experienced.
And fruit that was occasioned by good, or evil,
for you is not experienced.

dharmādharma-nimittaṃ vā
yadi te vidyate phalam |
dharmādharma-samutpannam
aśūnyaṃ te kathaṃ phalam |35|

sarva-saṃvyavahārāṃś ca
laukikān pratibādhase |
yat pratītya-samutpādam
śūnyatāṃ pratibādhase |36|

Or if, for you,
fruit occasioned by good or evil is experienced,
how, when it's being produced from good or evil,
is the fruit for you not empty?

Again, you are denying
all human efforts in the world,
when you deny dependent arising,
when you deny emptiness.

na kartavyaṃ bhavet kiṃ-cid
anārabdhā bhavet kriyā |
kārakaḥ syād akurvāṇaḥ
śūnyatāṃ pratibādhataḥ |*37*|

ajātam aniruddhaṃ ca
kūṭa-sthaṃ ca bhaviṣyati |
vicitrābhir avasthābhiḥ
svabhāve rahitaṃ jagat |*38*|

For one denying emptiness
nothing would be asking to be practised,
the work of practice would remain unbegun –
a case, perhaps, of the non-practising practitioner.

While existing unto itself,
the world will be without new growth
and without closure;
it'll be held rigid,
robbed of all its variegated situations.

asaṃprāptasya ca prāptir
duḥkha-paryanta-karma ca |
sarva-kleśa-prahāṇaṃ ca
yady aśūnyaṃ na vidyate |*39*|

yaḥ pratītya-samutpādaṃ
paśyatīdaṃ sa paśyati |
duḥkhaṃ samudayaṃ caiva
nirodhaṃ mārgam eva ca |*40*|

Coming into possession
of what's never been achieved;
action that ends suffering;
and dropping off all the afflictions,
if not empty is not experienced.

One who sees dependent arising sees this:
suffering,
its coming together,
its cessation
and, above all, a path.

nirvāṇa-parīkṣā

yadi śūnyam idaṁ sarvam

udayo nāsti na vyayaḥ |

prahāṇād vā nirodhād vā

kasya nirvāṇam iṣyate |1|

yady aśūnyam idaṃ sarvam

udayo nāsti na vyayaḥ |

prahāṇād vā nirodhād vā

kasya nirvāṇam iṣyate |2|

EXPLORING NIRVANA

[Opponent]

If all this is empty,
there is neither arising nor passing.
Through the dropping off
or through the inhibiting of what,
is nirvana sought?

If all this is not empty,
there is neither arising nor passing.
Through the dropping off
or through the inhibiting of what,
is nirvana sought?

aprahīṇam asaṃprāptam
anucchinnam aśāśvatam |
aniruddham anutpannam
etan nirvāṇam ucyate |3|

bhāvas tāvan na nirvāṇaṃ
jarā-maraṇa-lakṣaṇam |
prasajyetāsti bhāvo hi
na jarā-maraṇaṃ vinā |4|

What's not dropped off, or achieved;
what's not cut off, or eternal;
the uninhibited, and uninstigated –
this, happening here,
is called nirvana.

Nirvana, to begin with,
is not something that exists –
to which the mark of aging and dying might adhere.
For nothing that exists
is free from aging and dying.

bhāvaś ca yadi nirvāṇaṃ
nirvāṇaṃ saṃskṛtaṃ bhavet |
nāsaṃskṛto hi vidyeta
bhāvaḥ kva cana kaś cana |5|

bhāvaś ca yadi nirvāṇam
anupādāya tat katham |
nirvāṇaṃ nānupādāya
kaś-cid bhāvo hi vidyate |6|

If nirvana were something that existed,
nirvana would be confected.
For nowhere might any existent something be found
that wasn't confected.

Again, if nirvana were something that existed,
how would that going out of the fire
be free from clinging?
Without clinging, after all,
no existent something is witnessed.

bhāvo yadi na nirvāṇam
abhāvaḥ kiṃ bhaviṣyati |
nirvāṇaṃ yatra bhāvo na
nābhāvas tatra vidyate |*7*|

yady abhāvaś ca nirvāṇam
anupādāya tat katham |
nirvāṇaṃ na hy abhāvo 'sti
yo 'nupādāya vidyate |*8*|

If nirvana is not something that exists,
how will nirvana become an absence?
Where no existent something was,
no absence there is noticed.

If, again, nirvana were an absence,
how would that going out of the fire
be free from clinging?
Without clinging, after all,
whatever absence there is,
is not felt.

ya ājavaṃjavī-bhāva
upādāya pratītya vā |
so 'pratītyānupādāya
nirvāṇam upadiśyate |9|

prahāṇaṃ cābravic chāstā
bhavasya vibhavasya ca |
tasmān na bhāvo nābhāvo
nirvāṇam iti yujyate |10|

Whatever the hell is happening,
under the influence of clinging or conditioning,
that, without the clinging,
without the conditioning,
is taught as nirvana.

Again, the Teacher spoke
of a dropping off,
of the existent and of the nonexistent.
It works, on those grounds,
that nirvana is neither something existing
nor something not existing.

bhaved abhāvo bhāvaś ca
nirvāṇam ubhayaṃ yadi |
bhaved abhāvo bhāvaś ca
mokṣas tac ca na yujyate |*11*|

bhaved abhāvo bhāvaś ca
nirvāṇam ubhayaṃ yadi |
nānupādāya nirvāṇam
upādāyobhayaṃ hi tat |*12*|

If nirvana could happen
as something both existing and not existing,
coming undone could happen
as something existing and not existing.
But that is not workable.

If nirvana could happen
as something both existing and not existing,
going out of the fire
would not be free from clinging.
It would be a clinging on, in the end,
on both counts.

bhaved abhāvo bhāvaś ca
nirvāṇam ubhayaṃ katham |
asaṃskṛtaṃ hi nirvāṇaṃ
bhāvābhāvau ca saṃskṛtau |13|

bhaved abhāvo bhāvaś ca
nirvāṇa ubhayaṃ katham |
tayor abhāvo hy ekatra
prakāśa-tamasor iva |14|

How could nirvana happen
as something both existing and not existing?
For nirvana is unconfected,
whereas the duality of existent thing and absence
is dually confected.

How, in the fire going out,
could something's existence and absence
both be happening?
For those two not happening at one juncture
is like shining light and darkness.

naivābhāvo naiva bhāvo

nirvāṇam iti yā 'ñjanā |

abhāve caiva bhāve ca

sā siddhe sati sidhyati |15|

naivābhāvo naiva bhāvo

nirvāṇaṃ yadi vidyate |

naivābhāvo naiva bhāva

iti kena tad ajyate |16|

[Opponent]

Whatever proof there is that nirvana

is neither something that exists nor an absence,

that proof is established

only when both the existent thing and the absence

have been established.

If nirvana is witnessed

as neither something that exists nor an absence,

by what is it proved to be

neither the thing nor the absence?

paraṃ nirodhād bhagavān
bhavatīty eva nājyate |
na bhavaty ubhayaṃ ceti
nobhayaṃ ceti nājyate |*17*|

tiṣṭhamāno 'pi bhagavān
bhavatīty eva nājyate |
na bhavaty ubhayaṃ ceti
nobhayaṃ ceti nājyate |*18*|

It's not proved even that, after death,
a Glorious One is.
And it's not proved
that a Glorious One isn't.
Or both. Or neither.

Even while a Glorious One
is standing right there,
it's not proved
that a Glorious One is.
And it's not proved
that a Glorious One isn't.
Or both. Or neither.

na saṁsārasya nirvāṇāt
kiṁ-cid asti viśeṣaṇam |
na nirvāṇasya saṁsārāt
kiṁ-cid asti viśeṣaṇam |*19*|

nirvāṇasya ca yā koṭiḥ
koṭiḥ saṃsaraṇasya ca |
na tayor antaraṃ kiṃ-cit
susūkṣmam api vidyate |*20*|

Not the slightest thing exists in samsara
to distinguish it from nirvana.
Not the slightest thing exists in nirvana
to distinguish it from samsara.

Whatever is a highlight of nirvana
is a highlight also of samsara.
Between those two—
the fire going out and our wandering about—
not the slightest gap, even the tiniest one,
is witnessed.

paraṃ nirodhād antādyāḥ
śāśvatādyāś ca dṛṣṭayaḥ |
nirvāṇam aparāntaṃ ca
pūrvāntaṃ ca samāśritāḥ |*21*|

śūnyeṣu sarva-dharmeṣu
kim anantaṃ kim antavat |
kim antavac cānantam ca
nānantaṃ nāntavac ca kim |*22*|

Views about an end after death and suchlike,
and about eternity and suchlike,
are predicated on a future nirvana
and on a past one.

Where everything happening is empty,
what is without end?
What has an end?
What is both ending and endless?
And what is neither ending nor endless?

kiṃ tad eva kim anyat kiṃ
śāśvataṃ kim aśāśvatam |
aśāśvataṃ śāśvataṃ ca
kim vā nobhayam apy atha |23|

sarvopalambhopaśamaḥ
prapañcopaśamaḥ śivaḥ |
na kva-cit kasya-cit kaś-cid
dharmo buddhena deśitaḥ |24|

What actually is this? What else is there?
What is eternal? What is uneternal?
What is both eternal and uneternal?
Or else what, again, is neither?

Happiness is the melting away
of all conceptions,
the melting away of othering.
The Buddha did not teach
some dharma or other,
belonging to somebody,
happening somewhere.

dvādaśāṅga-parīkṣā

punar-bhavāya saṁskārān
avidyā-nivṛtas tridhā |
abhisaṁskurute yāṁs tair
gatiṁ gacchati karmabhiḥ |*1*|

vijñānaṁ saṁniviśate
saṁskāra-pratyayaṁ gatau |
saṁniviṣṭe 'tha vijñāne
nāma-rūpaṁ niṣicyate |*2*|

Veering towards yet another state of being,
one hampered by denial, in three ways,
repeatedly fabricates fabricated realities,
and by these doings
does go to a painful destination.

Into the painful realm
settles conditioned consciousness.
Then, divided consciousness having set in,
psycho-physicality is instilled.

niṣikte nāma-rūpe tu
ṣaḍāyatana-saṁbhavaḥ |
ṣaḍāyatanam āgamya
saṁsparśaḥ saṁpravartate |3|

cakṣuḥ pratītya rūpaṁ ca
samanvāhāram eva ca |
nāma-rūpaṁ pratītyaivaṁ
vijñānaṁ saṁpravartate |4|

But where psycho-physicality is instilled,
there's a coming together
of the sixfold sensorium.
The sixfold sensorium having arrived,
there occurs contact.

Depending on eyesight, on physicality,
and on the bringing of the two together –
depending in other words on psycho-physicality –
divided consciousness recurs.

saṁnipātas trayāṇāṁ yo
rūpa-vijñāna-cakṣuṣām |
sparśaḥ sa tasmāt sparśāc ca
vedanā saṁpravartate |5|

vedanā-pratyayā tṛṣṇā
vedanārthaṁ hi tṛṣyate |
tṛṣyamāṇa upādānam
upādatte catur-vidham |6|

Whatever concurrence there is of the three –
physicality, divided consciousness and eyesight –
that is contact;
and from that contact
there occurs feeling.

Conditioned by feeling, there's thirsting –
for the object of feeling is thirsted after.
While thirsting's going on,
clinging takes hold in the four ways.

upādāne sati bhava
upādātuḥ pravartate |
syādd hi yady anupādāno
mucyeta na bhaved bhavaḥ |*7*|

pañca skandhāḥ sa ca bhavo
bhavāj jātiḥ pravartate |
jarā-maraṇa-duḥkhādi
śokāḥ saparidevanāḥ |*8*|

Where there's clinging,
a state of being arises of the clinger,
for if he were free from clinging
he would come undone,
and being would not be.

The five aggregates are that state, again, of being.
Grounded in being
there occurs rebirth.
The suffering and so forth
of ageing and dying: sorrows,
accompanied by bewailing and complaining;

daurmanasyam upāyāsā

jāter etat pravartate |

kevalasyaivam etasya

duḥkha-skandhasya saṁbhavaḥ |*9*|

saṁsāra-mūlaṁ saṁskārān

avidvān saṁskaroty ataḥ |

avidvān kārakas tasmān

na vidvāṁs tattva-darśanāt |*10*|

...downheartedness, troubles –
all this arises out of rebirth.
In this way there's a coming together
of this whole aggregate of suffering.

Thus does one in denial,
rooted in errant states of existence,
fabricate fabricated realities.
That's how one in denial is a doer;
one who's wise is not,
through a realising of what's ineffable.

avidyāyāṁ niruddhāyāṁ
saṁskārāṇām asaṁbhavaḥ |
avidyāyā nirodhas tu
jñānasyāsyaiva bhāvanāt |*11*|

tasya tasya nirodhena
tat-tan nābhipravartate |
duḥkha-skandhaḥ kevalo 'yam
evaṁ samyag nirudhyate |*12*|

Where denial is being stopped,
fabrications do not happen.
But, stopping of denial, is,
in light of all of this,
through a letting happen.

With the stopping of each,
the others do not persist.
This whole aggregate of suffering in this way
is well and truly caused to cease.

dṛṣṭi-parīkṣā

abhūm atītam adhvānaṁ
nābhūvam iti dṛṣṭayaḥ |
yās tāḥ śāśvata-lokādyāḥ
pūrvāntaṁ samupāśritāḥ |*1*|

dṛṣṭayo na bhaviṣyāmi
kim anye 'nāgate 'dhvani |
bhaviṣyāmīti cāntādyā
aparāntaṃ samāśritāḥ |*2*|

EXPLORING VIEWS

Views that as a past iteration
I was there, or wasn't –
whatever views there are
that begin with a neverended world,
those views are predicated on a past.

Views that I will be no more
– Or will I be, in another life to come? –
views that begin with endings,
are predicated on a future.

abhūm atītam adhvānam
ity etan nopapadyate |
yo hi janmasu pūrveṣu
sa eva na bhavaty ayam |3|

sa evātmeti tu bhaved
upādānaṃ viśiṣyate |
upādāna-vinirmukta
ātmā te katamaḥ punaḥ |4|

That as a past iteration I was there
is not tenable, because,
whoever was there in previous births,
that same one has not become
this one now present.

That this self must,
on the contrary, be that same one,
means clinging has prevailed.
When your self is liberated from clinging
what self, in the end, do you have?

upādāna-vinirmukto
nāsty ātmeti kṛte sati |
syād upādānam evātmā
nāsti cātmeti vaḥ punaḥ |5|

na copādānam evātmā
vyeti tat samudeti ca |
kathaṃ hi nāmopādānam
upādātā bhaviṣyati |6|

It being given
that a self liberated from clinging
does not exist,
it might be, for you,
that a self is nothing but the clinging
so that, in the end, there is no self.

But clinging, as it passes and arises,
is not a self.
For how, pray, will the clinging
become the one who clings?

anyaḥ punar upādānād
ātmā naivopapadyate |
gṛhyeta hy anupādāno
yady anyo na ca gṛhyate |*7*|

evaṃ nānya upādānān
na copādānam eva saḥ |
ātmā nāsty anupādāno
nāpi nāsty eṣa niścayaḥ |*8*|

Still less does a self happen separately,
apart from clinging.
For if there were a separate one,
free from clinging,
one would be grasped,
and one is not grasped.

Thus it is not separate from clinging
and nor is it just the clinging.
There is no self free from clinging.
Neither is this one happening here
ascertained not to be.

nābhūm atītam adhvānam

ity etan nopapadyate |

yo hi janmasu pūrveṣu

tato 'nyo na bhavaty ayam |9|

yadi hy ayaṃ bhaved anyaḥ

pratyākhyāyāpi taṃ bhavet |

tathaiva ca sa saṃtiṣṭhet

tatra jāyeta cāmṛtaḥ |10|

That as a past iteration I wasn't there
is not tenable, because,
whoever was there in previous births,
someone other than that one
has not become this one now present.

For the other,
if it could become this one here,
might become so
even having disavowed it.
Equally, it might stay there and be born
without having died.

ucchedaḥ karmaṇāṃ nāśaḥ
kṛtam anyena karma ca |
pratisaṃvedayaty anya
evam ādi prasajyate |*11*|

nāpy abhūtvā samudbhūto
doṣo hy atra prasajyate |
kṛtako vā bhaved ātmā
sambhūto vāpy ahetukaḥ |*12*|

In this way would follow, for example,
nihilism, nullification of actions,
and causing the karma
one has created oneself
to be experienced by another.

Nor either,
without what happened having been endured,
did growth ever happen;
for from that would follow a fault –
a self might be created artificially
or else developed without cause.

evaṃ dṛṣṭir atīte yā
nābhūm aham abhūm aham |
ubhayaṃ nobhayaṃ ceti
naiṣā samupapadyate |*13*|

adhvany anāgate kiṃ nu
bhaviṣyāmīti darśanam |
na bhaviṣyāmi cety etad
atītenādhvanā samam |*14*|

Thus whatever view is there
haunting the past
– that an I wasn't or that an I was
or both or neither –
no such view stands up.

Whether I will be happening
or I won't be happening,
in a future iteration:
the same goes for this view
as for a past iteration.

sa devaḥ sa manuṣyaś ced

evaṃ bhavati śāśvatam |

anutpannaś ca devaḥ syāj

jāyate na hi śāśvatam |*15*|

devād anyo manuṣyaś ced

aśāśvatam ato bhavet |

devād anyo manuṣyaś cet

saṃtatir nopapadyate |*16*|

When man is God
thus does the eternal come to be.
And a God who's not arisen must exist
since what's eternal isn't caused to be.

When man is separate from God
the uneternal then is bound to be.
When man is separate from God
what can't occur is continuity.

divyo yady eka-deśaḥ syād
eka-deśaś ca mānuṣaḥ |
aśāśvataṃ śāśvataṃ ca
bhavet tac ca na yujyate |17|

aśāśvataṃ śāśvataṃ ca
prasiddham ubhayaṃ yadi |
sidhyen na śāśvataṃ kāmaṃ
naivāśāśvatam ity api |18|

If one part were human,
one part divine,
the uneternal and eternal
it would have to be.
But that is an impossibility.

If the uneternal and eternal
were both established
the view negating the uneternal and eternal
might also be readily established.

kutaś-cid āgataḥ kaś-cit
kiṃ-cid gacchet punaḥ kva-cit |
yadi tasmād anādis tu
saṃsāraḥ syān na cāsti saḥ |*19*|

nāsti cec chāśvataḥ kaś-cit
ko bhaviṣyaty aśāśvataḥ |
śāśvato 'śāśvataś cāpi
dvābhyām ābhyāṃ tiras-kṛtaḥ |*20*|

If someone coming from somewhere
were somehow to be going somewhere else
then samsara would exist all right
as the beginningless.
But he, she or it does not exist.

When no-one exists eternally
who will happen, non-eternally –
both eternally and uneternally even,
transcending this duality?

antavān yadi lokaḥ syāt
para-lokaḥ kathaṃ bhavet |
athāpy an-antavāl lokaḥ
para-lokaḥ kathaṃ bhavet |*21*|

skandhānām eṣa saṃtāno
yasmād dīpārciṣām iva |
tasmān nānantavattvaṃ ca
nāntavattvaṃ ca yujyate |*22*|

If this world had an ending,
how might a future world happen?
There again, if this world were endless,
how might a future world happen?

Because this continuity happening here
of constituents,
is like rays shining from a source
therefore neither ending nor endless fits.

pūrve yadi ca bhajyerann
utpadyeran na cāpy amī |
skandhāḥ skandhān pratītyemān
atha loko 'ntavān bhavet |23|

pūrve yadi na bhajyerann
utpadyeran na cāpy amī |
skandhāḥ skandhān pratītyemāl
loko 'nanto bhaved atha |24|

If, without those constituents there arising
dependent on these constituents here,
prior constituents could be broken up,
then this world would have endings.

If, without those constituents there
arising dependent on these constituents here,
prior constituents remained unbroken,
then this world would be endless.

antavān eka-deśaś ced
eka-deśas tv anantavān |
syād antavān anantaś ca
lokas tac ca na yujyate | *25* |

katham tāvad upādātur
eka-deśo vinaṅkṣyate |
na naṅkṣyate caika-deśa
evaṃ caitan na yujyate | *26* |

If one part had endings
while one part were endless
this world would be full of endings
and without end.
But that is not workable.

How here and now
could one part of the clinger
come to naught
while one part does not?
Such a thing also is unworkable.

upādānaika-deśaś ca
kathaṃ nāma vinaṅkṣyate |
na naṅkṣyate caika-deśo
naitad apy upapadyate |*27*|

antavac cāpy anantaṃ ca
prasiddham ubhayaṃ yadi |
sidhyen naivāntavat kāmaṃ
naivānantavad ity api |*28*|

And how, pray,
could one part of the clinging
come to naught
while one part does not?
This again is impossible.

If having ends and being endless
were both established
the view negating the ending and the endless
might also be readily established.

atha vā sarva-bhāvānāṃ
śūnyatvāc chāśvatādayaḥ |
kva kasya katamāḥ kasmāt
saṃbhaviṣyanti dṛṣṭayaḥ |*29*|

sarva-dṛṣṭi-prahāṇāya
yaḥ saddharmam adeśayat |
anukampām upādāya
taṁ namasyāmi gautamam |*30*|

And so on the grounds
of the emptiness of all happenings
where, for whom and how
will which views
– beginning with eternalism –
conspire to prevail?

He pointed to the happening dharma
Towards abandoning all views.
I bow to him, to Gautama,
Who of compassion made good use.

For further study of Nāgārjuna's
mūla-madhyamaka-kārikā (MMK)
– The Middle, in Root Verse –
Books One, Two and Three should follow soon:

Book One: Exploring
Chapters 1 to 8

Book Two: Continuing
Chapters 9 to 17

Book Three: Ending Denial
Chapters 18 to 23

Book Four: Cultivating
Chapters 24 to 27

The 108 verses forming this edition
are MMK's two dedicatory verses
plus the 106 verses of these last four chapters.

Printed in Great Britain
by Amazon

0020de8a-0395-4272-8300-fec075e96ecaR01